HOW TO BE A GREAT CHURCH USHER

All rights reserved. No part of this publication may be, distributed, or transmitted in any form or by any means, including; recording, or other electronic or mechanical methods, without the prior written permission of the publisher, except in the case of brief quotations embodied in critical reviews and certain other non-commercial uses permitted by copyright law.

For permission requests, write to the publisher, addressed "Attention: Permissions Coordinator," at the email address below.

Future Hope Legacy

London
England
admin@futurehopelegacy.com

www.futurehopelegacypublishing.com

Ordering Information:
Quantity sales. Special discounts are available on quantity purchases by ministries, churches, and others. For details, contact the publisher at the address above.
Orders by UK & U.S. trade bookstores and wholesalers.

Printed in the United Kingdom

How to be a GREAT Church Usher

Publisher's Cataloging-in-Publication data
Future Hope Legacy

Copyright © 2017 Future Hope Legacy

978-1-9998397-0-3

Appreciation

First and foremost, I thank my heavenly Father who continues to load me with benefits every day and has provided me with rich sources of inspiration, ideas, and the privilege of writing this book.

To Apostle C. Obaseki my dear husband – a strong man of God who has continually supported and encouraged my dreams and vision. He has never restricted my movements and has always believed in me even when I didn't believe in myself! Thank you, my darling.

To all the General Overseers, Pastors, Ministers, Leaders: past and present. All the experiences unsuspectingly fed me – the good, the bad and the ugly! I've used every experience to spur me on to my mission and channel it for good. So thank you!

Table of Contents

Introduction 1
How to use this workbook 5
Choosing an usher, meeter or greeter 7
How to maintain an usher, meeter, and greeter relationship 8
Who should teach this course? 11
What space and equipment is needed? 13
Front line worker ushers, ... 14
meeters, greeters 14
Front line worker ushers, meeters, greeters 21
Overview and Objectives - Week 1 22
Objectives - Week 1 22
What the Bible says about the ideal character of a Front Line Worker 23
What qualities should a 24
Front Line Worker possess? 24
 Conflict - Week 2 24
Objectives – Week 2 25
Review of Week 1 26
What causes conflict? 27
Dealing with conflict in a Godly Way 28
Role Description & Person Specification - Week 3 31
Review of Week 2 32
What should a Role Description include? 33
Example Role Description 34
Overview - Week 4 36
Practical Service Training - Week 4 37
Practical Service Training 38
Week 4 (part 2) 38

Introduction

2Timothy 3:17

Why Training for Church Ushers?

I wrote this workbook having been an usher, then Head of Ushers. I then served as the Head of the Training Department later in my ministerial career, and noticed the scarcity of training and development ushers received.

It occurred to me that in any given company, you'd never employ Customer Service Representatives without first training them, after all they are usually the first to meet or greet customers. First impressions count in any sphere, and the local church is no exception to that rule.

I've experienced a poor reception in some churches at the hands of some ushers. It seems no one told them what to do and how to do it, so they made their own rules up.

I will never forgot the time I was sitting at the back of the church to observe the Ushers in the church I served in, with a view to developing some training for them.

A young couple I'd never seen before entered, both looking particularly stressed. One of the ushers approached them. I didn't hear what was said, but from the usher's gestures she seemed to be instructing them to move in a fairly forthright way. Please note that the seat didn't have a reserved sign and there was no Usher standing close enough to direct them anywhere else. I heard the lady of the couple state very aggressively, *'I'm not coming back where I'm not welcome'*, and with that picked up her bag and left. The young man had no choice but to follow her. I ran down the stairs trying to convince them otherwise, but it was too late, the damage was done. I never saw them in the church again. It turned out that the Usher in question was new to the section and had not even completed a Foundational Membership Class. The rules were already in place to ensure no labourer was allowed to serve in a department, until they'd completed the course. Somehow was put on the 'Front Line' with devastating results.

Yes, ushering is a very important role for the local church and needs to be handled with more respect. That young couple may or may not have been saved, we may never know. We can't afford to loose souls for God's Kingdom especially in this secular society we live in.

I am passionate about good service. No matter where you go or what you do, if you receive good service you are likely to return. Ushering, meeting and greeting (I like to refer to it as Front Line Work) is a ministry and also a spiritual customer service role. I call those involved Front Line Workers because they are the first point of contact in a church or ministry. Not everyone is cut out for this role. But those who possess a passion for welcoming people have a gift, even a calling. This attribute should never be underestimated or looked down upon; it is an important role in ministries and the church.

I liken ushering to a shop window. If people don't like what's on display in the shop, they won't walk in. Similarly, if you do enter the shop and are met by a person with a cold or disinterested attitude, you'll vote with your feet! In the same vein, church visitors may decide not to come back because as the old adage says, "You don't get a second chance at a first impression!"

This is a 4-week course for church ushers, meeters, and greeters. The workbook is laid out as a step-by-step guide for teachers and includes a teaching/lesson plan, exercises, and information for students. It shares tried and tested tips as well as a structure for a course you can run in your church for large or small groups of ushers/meeters or greeters.

The subjects covered are:

- What qualities ushers, meeters or greeters should possess
- How to deal with conflict
- Role Description for ushers, meeters or greeters
- Practical in-service training

Generally, in the church training in this area is often overlooked. Some may perceive that it takes too much time to plan and deliver while others may feel it will make no difference. Many underestimate the power of training and nurturing Front Line Workers and, indeed, any worker!

2 Timothy 3:17 says, "*So that the servant of God[a] may be thoroughly equipped for every good work.*" Training will help all the

labourers in the vineyard to reach that goal and prepare them to operate at a high level of competence.

It's a proven fact that training volunteers is beneficial to the church and the individual. Most labourers in the vineyard are unpaid volunteers and I believe there should be non-monetary incentives to keep them motivated and engaged in the ministry and its vision. Training also ensures that all workers follow the same system and pattern of working, leading to less confusion and more efficiency. Thus, better communication and ultimately, a better experience for the church visitor or member.

Training does not have to take up too much time if it's organised at set times, over set periods. You do need named people to deliver the training; however, a variety of individuals can also be included:

Senior Minister or **any Minister** or **Leader** depending on your organisational structure

Head of Ushers Department

Deputy Head Ushers Department (if there is one),

A **Training Officer** (if your ministry has one)

A combination of the aforementioned.

I've delivered training to a combination of the aforementioned with equal success, though it does require the prior briefing and organisation of teachers. If we're to win souls, every aspect of ministry is important including the much-maligned usher, meeter or greeter role.

How to use this workbook

Tutorial Pack

The tutorial pack in this workbook provides you with a detailed guide on how to structure your sessions with a Lesson Plan for each week.

The pack is clearly split into 4 weeks with objectives for each week and Tutorial/Teacher notes for Weeks 1-4 set out in separate tables for each week.

What to provide for your students

Provide or ask students to bring along their notebooks and pens for group exercises.

If you have an **organisational chart** for your church, prepare it for Week 13 so that your ushers/meeters/greeters understand the structure and where they fit into the ministry as a whole.

In addition, if your church has a **Mission Statement** or **Vision Statement**, it would be very useful to share it. As the Bible states in Proverbs 29:18: *"Without vision my people perish."'* Involve your workers in the ministry of Vision and Mission, so they know where they fit in and how they can contribute to fulfilling the goals of the church or ministry.

After the course

Keep a record of the training delivered for each individual on your database.

If your church does not use a database, prepare a simple spreadsheet confirming units/weeks attended and the outcomes.

It's good practice to present attendance certificates after the course so people feel they've achieved something worthwhile.

Wherever possible, arrange to present the certificates publicly i.e. at one of the fellowship services on a Saturday or Sunday, and ask the Senior Pastor, Leader in Charge or Senior Minister to present them. This will validate the efforts of your students and help inspire potential labourers in the vineyard.

How to use the student section in this book

You can use the materials in this book by photocopying relevant sections for each of your ushers/meeters/greeters for each week of the course.

Provide a folder for them to keep their work notes in.

Choosing an usher, meeter or greeter

1. Announce your need for ushers, meeters and greeters

Inform the congregation that you're looking for ushers, meeters or greeters and let them know who to contact.

Ask each "applicant" to fill in a simple form with their basic details and confirmation they are interested in the usher role.

2. Carry out a selection interview

Since the role is all about communication skills, it's worth having an informal interview.

The interview does not have to be formal, but it ensures the right person for the role.

Successful candidates are more likely to take their roles seriously as a result of a formal interview because they had to qualify for the positions.

Use the role description (you'll find an example in Week 3) to tailor the interview questions; this will help you identify if the person has the right competencies and temperament.

How to maintain an usher, meeter, and greeter relationship

1. Induction

What's an induction? It is a formal introduction to the ministry/church. Most new appointees whether in a secular company or ministry stand or fall in the first few weeks based on the quality of their induction.

Induction is crucial because the ground rules are established. These include the preferred approach at your local church as prescribed by leaders or the vision/mission statement. Departmental rules and regulations, health and safety practices, team introductions etc. are established in the first few weeks. I have seen perfectly good candidates fall by the wayside because of the lack or quality of the induction. Prepare a pack for new ushers, meeters, and greeters documenting the what, where, when, how and why or as I like to call it the "dos and don'ts."

2. Provide Training & Development

This book provides that very opportunity! Training is a motivator for workers who do not receive payments to carry out their tasks. I believe they need non-financial incentives and motivation to keep them enthused and engaged. More on that below.

Assign responsibility for key areas of work to your ushers. This includes preparation before and after each service or event. The advantage of giving workers areas of responsibility is to encourage them to see themselves as stakeholders – they feel "at one" with the ministry mission and ethos. The desired result should be to have focused workers who are excellent all round. However, these systems need to be embedded in the whole structure.

3. Appraise usher performance regularly

The line managers (i.e. whoever the ushers, meeters, and greeters report to), need to ensure that they evaluate and appraise performances on a regular basis. On an informal basis, this should happen weekly as they observe performances. The line manager needs to be prepared to correct any shortcomings but also, equally important, praise good work and practices. Always give feedback like a good sandwich: the good, the not so good, and end on a good note, so the workers don't end up feeling deflated.

On a formal basis, you should do evaluations every 6 months, which is ideally twice yearly, but definitely every year.

4. Include a non-financial incentive

As previously discussed, keeping any unpaid volunteer motivated is the key to maintaining any relationship. Here are some great worker incentive ideas:

Why not introduce something they feel they can look forward to?

Usher of the month (or you could run it quarterly), would be fun and can be voted by the general congregation or laity. Collect each winner over the year and give an usher of the year award with a special celebration.

Provide more than one person an opportunity to be recognised. In fact, you can have more than one award with different names. For example

- The Usher Who Smiles the Most Award
- The Smartest Dressed Usher Award
- The Most Punctual Usher Award

Make it fun so people want to be involved. As a Training and Organisational Development Leader at my local church, these are incentives administered by my department. However, your Administration Team or the Usher Team themselves could easily organise these initiatives. They do not have to be expensive; it's the thought that counts. However, once you start, it is important to keep up the momentum or people will lose confidence.

Who should teach this course?

Any of the following can teach this course:

Head or Lead Usher

Church Training Officer/Leader

Pastor or **Minister** with previous experience of ushering, meeting or greeting or a clear idea of what is required.

How long is the course?

This course is designed to run for 4 weeks with a minimum 1 hour per week (ideally 1.5 hours if this can be fitted in) OR it could be run 1 FULL day with breaks in between, including practical Service Training.

I have run these sessions on Sundays after service with refreshments provided. I have also run them on Saturdays FULL day. It really depends on what's possible in your local church.

The Tutor/Teacher should ensure that the preparation for each section is done in advance. He /She should be in the classroom or teaching session at least 15mins before each session starts.

Recording Attendance and Managing Discipline

You will be dealing mainly with adults ideally people over 18 years old so the need for discipline will probably not be necessary (at least, one would think so!). However, it's important to set the right professional tone.

Brief students before the course starts letting them know the times they are expected to attend, what happens if they are late etc. Keep a register to track attendance. You might want to enforce a rule on the minimum amount of attendance days too.

It is no good if they miss half the course; they will have learnt half of what they need to learn!

Who is the course for?

New and existing volunteers or paid Front Line Workers i.e. Ushers/Meeters and Greeters and even Protocol/Security staff would benefit. Basically, anyone who is in a hospitality role within the church.

What space and equipment is needed?

If you don't have the luxury of classroom training space, you can set up in a corner of your church. Just find a table and as many chairs as you need. Try to use a room with daylight where at all possible and/or good ventilation. You'll need a **flip chart** or **data projector** (if you choose to show PowerPoint slides). The use of visual aids provides contrast and continued interest for your students.

Use the space you hold your weekly services in for Week 4s Practical Service training to ensure workers know exactly where they place items and the drill.

Try to provide drinking water. If arranging this training on a full day on Saturday, offer light refreshments as your workers have given up their time to attend the training.

Front line worker ushers, meeters, greeters

4 WEEK COURSE OVERVIEW/SYLLABUS

WEEK 1: What qualities should a Front Line Worker (Usher, Meter, Greeter) possess?

WEEK 2: What causes conflict?

WEEK 3: Role Description and Person Specification – What role does a Front Line Worker do and what sort of person would be ideal?

WEEK 4: Practical hands-on session – onsite service training

HOW TO BE A GREAT CHURCH USHER

Tutorial Lesson Plan – One hour or Part of a Full Day

WEEK 1 - THE IDEAL QUALITIES OF A FRONT LINE WORKER

SUBJECT	MINUTES	VISUAL AIDS	TUTORIAL INSTRUCTIONS/COMMNENTS
PRAYER	5mins	None	Tutor to lead prayer
Objectives and Overview of session	5mins	Presentation showing overview and objectives	Tutor to Lead
What the Bible says about the character of a Front Line Worker	10mins	Bible	Ask delegates to read Galatians 5:22-23 (Fruit of the Spirit) and discuss
Ideal qualities of a Front Line Worker	15mins	Flip Chart or Post-it Notes	<ul><li>Divide Groups into syndicates</li><li>Ask groups to write the qualities of Front Line Workers</li><li>Groups to report on their findings</li></ul>
Ideal qualities of a Front Line Worker	10mins	Flip Chart or Post-it Notes	<ul><li>Display flip chart or post-it notes</li><li>Discuss and compare ideas from students with those in the presentation</li></ul>
Reporting Line/Chain of Command	10mins	Show your ministry Organisational Chart if you have one OR discuss reporting line i.e. who reports to whom across the entire ministry	<ul><li>Tutor, to discuss what a reporting line is.</li><li>Why is a reporting line important?</li><li>Who should ushers report to and for what reason?</li></ul>
Discuss week 2 homework – Conflict	5mins	None	Ask students to make a list of what they feel causes conflict amongst groups
PRAYER	5mins	None	Tutor to lead

	Tutorial Lesson Plan– One hour or Part of a Full Day WEEK 2 – CONFLICT		
SUBJECT	MINUTES	VISUAL AIDS	TUTORIAL INSTRUCTIONS/COMMNENTS
PRAYER	5mins	None	Tutor to lead prayer
Objectives and Overview of session	5mins	Presentation Slides	Tutor to lead
Review Week 1	10mins	Notes from Week 1	Ask random open questions to test the learning of the ideal qualities of a Front Line Worker from Week 1
Homework Conflict	10mins	Flip Chart or Post-it Notes	Ask students about their ideas on conflict amongst workers
Conflict	15mins	Presentation	Share presentation/diagram on conflict and compare student answers to those on diagram & how to avoid conflict
Preparation for Week 3 – what role do you do?	5mins	None	Ask students to list their duties AND the ideal qualities/personalities that are also known as Person Specification i.e. the ideal person for the role

Tutorial Lesson Plan – One hour or Part of a Full Day

WEEK 3 – ROLE DESCRIPTION AND PERSON SPECIFICATION

SUBJECT	MINUTES	VISUAL AIDS	TUTORIAL INSTRUCTIONS/COMMNENTS
PRAYER	5mins	None	Tutor to lead prayer
Objectives and Overview of session	5mins	Presentation Slides	Tutor to lead
Review Week 2	10mins	Notes from Week 2	Ask random open questions to test the learning of Conflict from Week 2
Homework – What role do you do?	10mins	None	Ask students about their ideas on Role Description & Person Specification
What do Front Line Workers i.e. Ushers, Meeters and Greeters do?	15mins	Example Role Description with Person Specification	Share Example Role Description and discuss Person Specification (use Week 1 – Qualities of a Front Line worker to help your students understand what a Person Specification is).
What role do you do?	10mins	None	Ask students to list the content of their roles and the ideal qualities and personalities of a Front Line Worker

HOW TO BE A GREAT CHURCH USHER

Tutorial Lesson Plan– Two hours or Part of a Full Day				
WEK 4 – PRACTICAL SERVICE TRAINING			
SUBJECT	MINUTES	VISUAL AIDS	TUTORIAL INSTRUCTIONS/COMMENTS
PRAYER	5mins	None	Students to lead prayer if appropriate
Objectives and Overview of Session	5mins	None	Tutor to lead
Review of Week 3	10mins	Role Description is drawn up from Week 3	Ask random questions regarding their roles and agree on what they think they should be doing before, during and after the service
Preparation before each service	15mins	Role Description is drawn up from Week 3	Ask students to agree on exactly what needs to be done before service and who will be responsible
Order of Service	15mins	Copy of your church/ministry order of service	Discuss what students should be doing during each part of the service.
BREAK	15MINS	BREAK	BREAK
Positioning	15mins	Copy of your church/ministry order of service	Agree on strategic positions for ushers/meeters/greeters, relevant to each part of the Order of Service
Drilling	15-20mins	Copy of your church/ministry order of service	Select a key part of the service e.g. "Offering collection" and practice drilling and positioning with students in the location the service takes place.

Student Evaluation

USHER MEETER AND GREETER TRAINING

1. Did you feel the training was worthwhile?

    YES   NO

    If you answered NO to Question 1, please state why below

    _____

    _____

2. Were the lessons easy to follow?   YES NO

3. What was your favourite part of the training?
   _____

4. What would you do differently if you were running the workshop?
   _____

   _____

THANK YOU! PLEASE HAND THIS INTO YOUR TUTOR

HOW TO BE A GREAT CHURCH USHER

Front Line Workers Training

Student Workbook

Ushers, Meeters & Greeters

Front line worker ushers, meeters, greeters

4 WEEK COURSE OVERVIEW/SYLLABUS

- What qualities and behaviours should a Front Line Worker (Usher/Meter Greeter) adopt?

- What tasks are Front Line Workers responsible for?

- What sort of character should a Front Line Worker have?

- What duties should a Front Line Worker carry out?

- PLUS Practical hands on session – onsite service training

Overview and Objectives - Week 1

Qualities of a Front Line Worker

PRAYER
Introductions
Objectives of the session
The Character of Front Line Worker – Galatians 5: 22 & 23
Qualities of Front Line Workers – Group Exercise/Syndicate Work
The ministry Leadership Reporting Line/Chain of Command; What is it? Who's involved? Why is it SO important?
Homework – FOR Week 2 – Research, discuss and explore - what causes conflict?
PRAYER

Objectives - Week 1

Ideal qualities of a Front Line worker

At the end of the session delegates will:

Understand the ideal qualities which a Front Line Worker (Usher/Meter Greeter) should possess for ministry

What the Bible says about the ideal character of a Front Line Worker

> "But the fruit of the Spirit is Love, Joy, Peace, Forbearance, Kindness, Goodness, Faithfulness, Gentleness and Self-Control. Against such things, there is no law. 24 Those who belong to Christ Jesus have crucified the flesh with its passions and desires. 25 Since we live by the Spirit, let us keep in step with the Spirit. 26 Let us not become conceited, provoking and envying each other" (Galatians 5: 22-23).

When you deal with people from different kinds of backgrounds, cultures, education or experiences, there is bound to be some conflict.

But verse 24 of Galatians 5, tells us that "Those who belong to Christ Jesus, have crucified the flesh with its passions and desires."

Our natural human instincts might want us to lash out or respond in negative ways towards someone who may be rude to us, abrupt, curt, angry etc. For example, when you direct visitors to their seats and they refuse. In such situations, try to understand what might be behind the refusal/attitude. As a Front Line worker, you should do as the verse says: crucify the flesh and ask the Holy Spirit to take control of your reactions. If you follow that pattern, you will always be in control of what you say and how you react.

What qualities should a Front Line Worker possess?

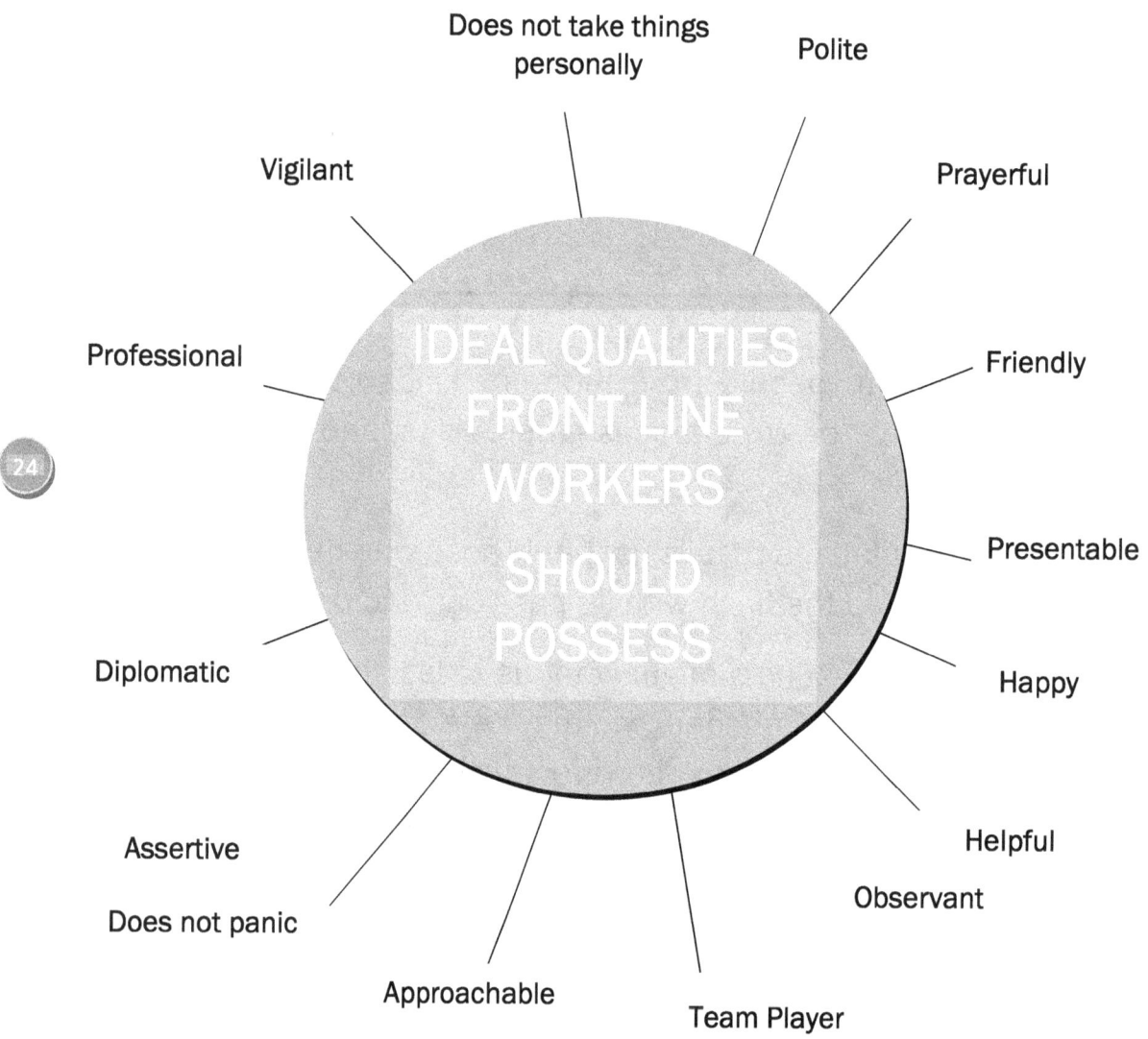

Conflict - Week 2

PRAYER
REVIEW OF WEEK 1 – How much do students remember?
What causes conflict? – SHARE IDEAS FROM HOMEWORK GIVEN – Group Exercise/discussion
Share the conflicting image
PREPARATION FOR WEEK 3 – Job Descriptions and Person Specifications
PRAYER

Objectives – Week 2

At the end of the session delegates will:

Understand the ideal qualities a Front Line Worker (Usher/Meeter Greeter) should possess for ministry

Review of Week 1

What did we talk about in Week 1?

What key things did you learn or were you reminded of?

What improvements do you think you can make or have started to make since the last session?

What causes conflict?

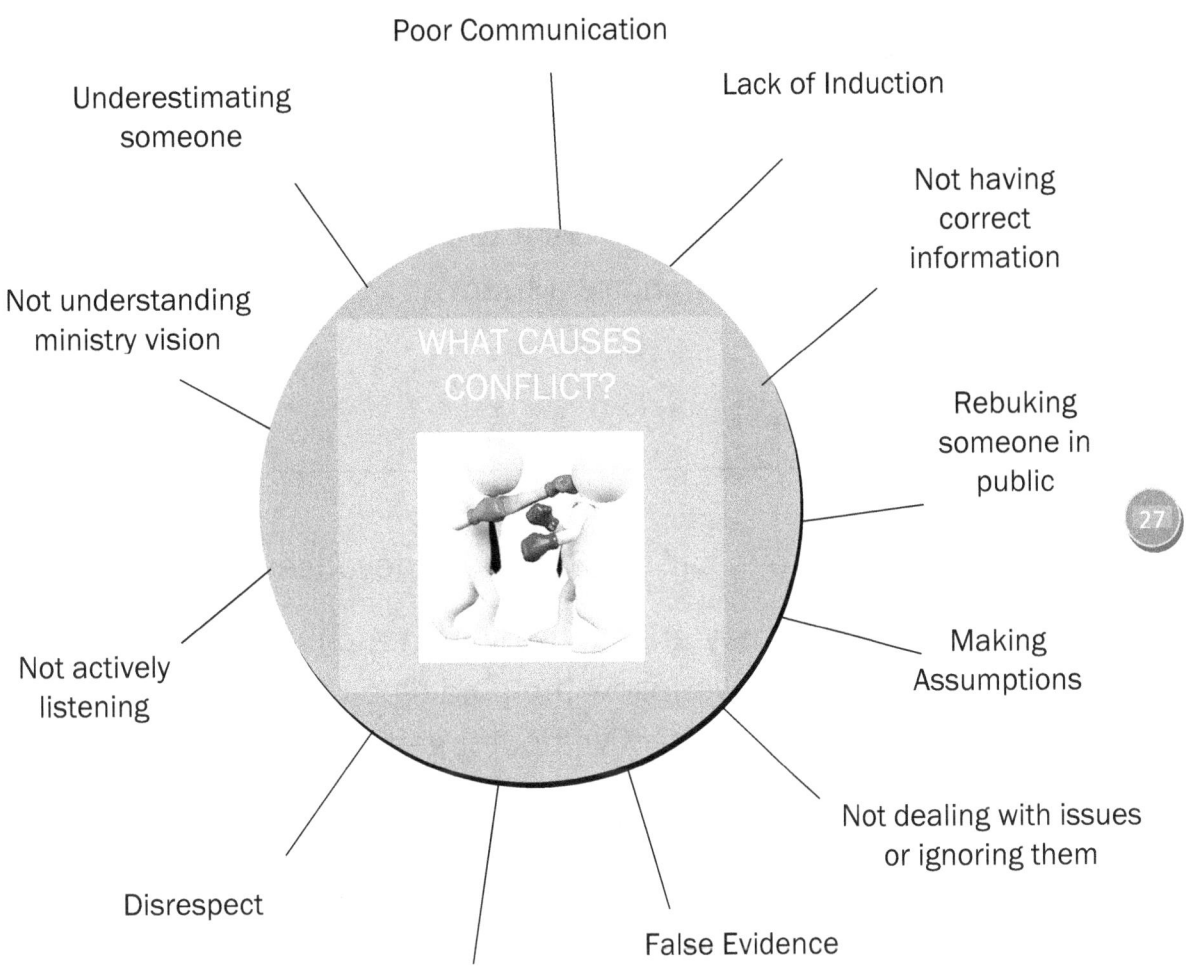

Dealing with conflict in a Godly Way

> ¹⁵ "If your brother or sister sins, go and point out their fault, just between the two of you. If they listen to you, you have won them over
>
> ¹⁶ But if they will not listen, take one or two others along, so that 'every matter may be established by the testimony of two or three witnesses.'
>
> ¹⁷ If they still refuse to listen, tell it to the church; and if they refuse to listen even to the church, treat them as you would a pagan or a tax collector
>
> (Matthew 18: 15-17)

This is what we like to call the Spiritual Grievance Procedure!

In teams, conflicts may arise (yes even in a church – especially in a church!). However, if we follow the guidelines as laid out in Matthew 18, we can deal with conflict without it getting out of hand.

The key points to dealing with conflict:

- Speak to the person you feel has offended you face to face or one on one. Avoid involving a third party at this stage, unless one of the persons involved is inexperienced or junior in which case it would be advantageous.

- Make sure you are listening actively to each other without interruption.

- Agree on a way forward and how to handle certain situations in the future to avoid further conflict.

However, if you feel there has been no resolution then you need to escalate your complaint to someone who has authority over you/your colleague. By all means make sure this is dealt with, because like disease it an spread and cause more damage.

Conflict from visitors

As an usher and then a departmental head of the usher team, I can tell you, I've experienced all sorts of behaviour from visitors. It really takes grace to do this work, however insight will assist you in communicating more effectively and avoiding some of the effects of conflict. As I have said throughout prayer should also play a major role to facilitate your work. It really helps.

Someone once asked me if we can avoid conflict. My answer was, if you say nothing and do nothing yes! Because our needs, background and upbringing are usually different, we can respond, react or behave differently. What one man or woman perceives as a friendly welcome, another can observe as suspicious possibly because of their past experiences. The other factor to consider is they may not yet know God for themselves. They may even be from a different religion or previously had no belief. There are many factors the make people behave the way they do.

When a visitor walks into your church, you don't know what they have been going through or currently experiencing. They may respond in an outwardly aggressive manner to your request to sit in a seat you have earmarked for them. That may be aggressive words or body language. The key is not to rise to it. On the other hand a visitor may appear withdrawn or outwardly shy. As time progresses your prayer should include one to enable you to be discerning. It will assist with better communication.

Sometimes the rules and regulations have to take a back step to relationship building in order to understand what you might be dealing with. For example, some have come from a life where they might dress in a way that suits them, but may not fit into your church environment. We need to handle this with tact and diplomacy. If they knew better they would do better. By understanding and stretching the hand of love and fellowship, they will gradually learn by good examples set from you and your colleagues.

One final thought on conflict. There is no traction without friction. A wheel needs friction in order for it to turn. Because we are all different we are not always going to have the same view point, so at times we will encounter conflict. However, if we make a decision to handle it the Godly way there will be no need for animosity in the long term.

Role Description & Person Specification - Week 3

Overview

Prayer
Review of Week 2
Reminder of what causes conflict
How can you avoid conflict
What is a job description?
What duties do you perform?
What's a person specification?
Prayer

Objectives

By the end of the session students will:

Understand ideal personal qualities and skills for Front Line Worker

Review of Week 2

TEAM TASK PART 1 - Think about your role as an usher, and what it is you actually do?

List them as a team.

TEAM TASK PART 2 - As a team, list the ideal personal qualities of a meeter/greeter (use Week 1 for clues) e.g. calm, polite etc.

You have 10 minutes!!

What should a Role Description include?

Usher/Meter & Greeter

Purpose of your Role

How will you look? i.e. what you will wear

What duties will you perform?

What behaviours will you adopt?

Protocol

Purpose of your role:

What duties will you perform?

What behaviours will you adopt?

How will you look?

NOTE FOR Head/Deputy – use this information to draw up a Role Description for all Ushers and Protocol Team Members

Example Role Description

Some duties may vary from in some local churches and denominations

Role Purpose – Usher

Meet and greet all who come into the church with welcoming smile and friendly helpful manner, directing them to the most suitable seats.

Deal with any general enquiries or direct to suitable worker

Preparation before service

1. Wear prescribed uniform/colours clothing as directed by Deputy Head or Head of Department
2. Ensure auditorium and accessible areas are clean and tidy including toilets checking for stock and replenishing
3. Collect any related documentation before service
4. Assist in sales of items as people arrive
5. Distribute offering envelopes/programmes etc.

Whilst Service is ongoing

1. Ensure safety or individuals
2. Keeping noise levels low/limiting movement
3. Assist in crowd control during offering and/or tithe
4. Help anyone with limited mobility or needing help
5. Hand out visitors cards to newcomers
6. Assist (cashiers) if required to collect offering baskets

After Service

1. Manage general enquiries and act as a signposting service
2. Assist with any administrative tasks connected with the service
3. Assist in sell media and other merchandise
4. Clear working area ready for next service

Person Specification for usher meeter/greeter

Polite warm and welcoming - essential

Responsive, quick - essential

Organised - desirable

Respectful to all - essential

Able to volunteer with and liaise with other departments as necessary – Desirable

Interdepartmental Relationships (this will vary from church to church)

Media team, Protocol (if there is one), Administration Team

External Relationships

New Visitors

Reports to

Deputy Head of (Meter/Greeters, Ushers) OR Head of (Meters/Greeters, Ushers)

Overview - Week 4

Frontline Worker – Practical Service Training

What is Service Training?

This is the practical application in the form of role play in the place where services take place. Ushers, meeters and greeters are taken through every access of the service from beginning to end to ensure everyone knows what they are supposed to do for each service.

AIM of the Training

To improve the perception and experience of all visitors and members of the ministry

Objectives of the Session

For all Ushers, Protocol to gain a thorough understanding of duties to be performed in each service using practical on-site exercises and examples & role play

Session Time – 2 hours (with break in between)

Practical Service Training - Week 4

NB: Preparation before the service - If you don't have a role description with a list of duties, use the example we've provided as a starting point/guide. Add duties particular to your ministry to provide a comprehensive list.

Below are a few examples:

Prayer – Each Usher/Meter and Greeter should meet on each day of service beforehand and pray for God's control over the service, His abiding presence, protection etc.

Check Auditorium, hall/room/area is clean and tidy – remove any objects which can harm

Check Toilet/Lavatory/Bathroom area for cleanliness, enough stock and flag up any issues to the cleaning team

Cordon off an area for nursing mothers, towards back of the auditorium

Ensure area reserved for **Ministers, Pastors** etc. by preparing or locating reserved labels/signs.

Ensure there are **Enough Envelopes** or **Collection Plates** for offering

Ensure **Tithe Cards** (if you use them in your church), **Offering Baskets or similar** are in the right position

Dress Code – This should be checked/agreed the week before each service and agreed by the head or deputy. It's worth working out a full month at a time for this or agreeing on standard weekly uniforms in the rotation. If there's a special event, a suggestion is to work out what might coordinate with the theme in line with your ministry's branding.

Practical Service Training

Week 4 (part 2)

Preparation BEFORE the service

1. Discuss and demonstrate appropriate ways of meeting and greeting visitors

2. Discuss and study the order of service and special directions

3. Head or Deputy – allocate positions for ushers, meeters, and greeters from the entrance to the auditorium

4. Drill and practice a sequence/process for Crowd Control, Offering, and Altar Call etc.

5. Discuss arrangements and duties required after the service and who should be responsible for them

www.ingramcontent.com/pod-product-compliance
Lightning Source LLC
Chambersburg PA
CBHW081504070526
44586CB00019B/2469